Back 4 Blood

The Complete Guide & Walkthrough with Tips &Tricks

Tips and Tricks

Fundamental Tips and Tricks for Getting Started in Back 4 Blood

Searching for something specifically? Snap the connections underneath to leap to...

Quick Tips and Tricks

Combat Tips and Tricks

Exploration Tips and Tricks

Speedy Tips and Tricks

Take note of the various sorts of harm that Back 4 Blood has to bring to the table. This is what you need to know Solid red harm can be recuperated by swathes and medkits.

Black and red harm is known as injury harm and can't be recuperated by ordinary means. To fix injury harm you need to track down a medical aid station, which are commonly locked behind supply reserves that require a tool stash to open.

Blue wellbeing, which is gotten basically by utilizing pain relievers, can mend injury harm, yet it's just transitory wellbeing. It will exhaust by one each several seconds until everything's gone.

Have your sounds turned up, as tuning in for sound prompts, for example, resting commotions and spewing can truly give your group the advantage. Knowing about an adversary's area before you get the opportunity to outwardly spot them can truly be a distinct advantage to how your group approach specific circumstances going ahead.

Don't ignore the advantages of stacking a couple of expanded endurance or ammunition cards, particularly when initially beginning, as having the option to surpass or cut down swarms longer can be vital for endurance.

Toolkits are an unquestionable requirement, particularly on the off chance that you anticipate investigating secret regions! So when your group is restocking supplies, ensure something like one partner has a tool stash close by. Regardless of the circumstance, a tool compartment ought to consistently take need.

Communication is the way in to your group's accomplishment in Back 4 Blood. Regardless of whether it's bringing down adversaries together, sharing updates and supplies, or in any event, something as basic as investigating, the way in work your group cooperates will at last decide how well your group gets by during each game.

Wondering off alone is quite often a surefire capital punishment. So to repeat above, consistently stay with your group and make certain to impart your developments in case you're needing to investigate new regions.

Nests will hinder your advancement until you annihilate all the developments and hubs - if all else fails, follow the sparkling red ringlets to discover the hubs that should be obliterated.

Better extraordinariness weapons implies better details, so it's quite often worth trading out a typical beginning weapon for something better down the line.

Both your fundamental weapon and sidearm can have mods on them. While you can't eliminate a mod, you can supplant it with new mods you find or purchase in the protected room. This will drop your old mod on the ground, so either let a partner prepare it, or trade to your sidearm and put the old mod on it.

Certain weapons you discover will have red-shaded mods. These are harmed and have negative modifiers, so be keeping watch for new mods to supplant them.

Be keeping watch for all around set gas bottles, as when shot, they'll cause an enormous blast, taking out any close by foes that are inside its span.

A red region will be shown when holding down toss,

demonstrating the shoot range of the thing you are holding. This impact sweep is particularly useful when you need a thing to be tossed in a particular region.

The request of your cards matters, so request them appropriately. The card put at the highest point of the deck will be your beginning card, so you'll have to guarantee that your cards are recorded arranged by significance as the higher the card, the prior you'll be offered it.

Need assistance arranging your deck? Our Best Cards and Combinations Guide will detail a portion of our number one cards on offer, alongside mixes for each circumstance and playstyle.

Back 4 Blood - 7 Deck Building Tips From the Developers

Battle Tips and Tricks

Almost all foes have sparkling weakspots, so make certain to focus on these spaces, as you'll bargain additional harm for each effective hit.

Make sure to organize your ammunition types. Having an excessive number of players all utilizing a similar ammunition type will make you run out of ammunition rapidly since your colleagues will all be battling for a similar ammunition.

On that equivalent note, in case you're low on ammunition, inquire as to whether they have any extra ammunition for a firearm they're not utilizing. You can drop ammunition by raising your stock and hauling the ammunition you need to drop off the menu.

Use your skirmish slam expertise to push zombies off of you while you reload. Slamming doesn't interfere with your reload, so you can push adversaries away and reload all simultaneously.

It's not difficult to get overpowered in Back 4 Blood, particularly as gigantic crowds of zombies swarm you. Therefore, we strongly suggest focusing on the request in which you bring down foes. Managing bigger targets like Tallboys, Stingers, and Hockers, ought to consistently be your principle center, as these adversaries sneak up all of a sudden and have been known to rapidly wipe groups that have had their concentrate somewhere else.

Investigation Tips and Tricks

Whatever you do, don't surprise the herds of birds that you'll discover dissipated all through each guide, as when scared, they'll alert any close by zombie swarms straightforwardly to your area.

Be mindful of your environmental elements, as you'll regularly discover hints around the conditions that you are investigating, for example, signs, showing that alerts have been set up. So, make certain to twofold and possibly significantly increase check those vehicles and neglected structure entryways before you go charging in.

Keep an eye out for Intel Folders frequently found in structures, as they'll either allow every player to get a free dynamic card, or now and then spend coins to get an all the more impressive card.

Have something like one colleague get the card to detect close by cash and assign them as the one to investigate while others ensure them.

Cars will frequently contain cash and once in a while even help things - however may expect you to break a few windows.

While we don't suggest severing from your gathering, you will regularly discover Copper stashes off the principle way. In this way, reassuring your group to take outside of what might be expected may once in a while enjoy its benefits.

You can climb and mantle more territory than you may

might suspect - having the key position is consistently a reward, so attempt to discover more responsible options however much as could reasonably be expected to remain one stride in front of the crowds.

Searching for much more Back 4 Blood content? Why not look at our total Campaign Walkthrough or the Best Cards and Combinations you ought to think about when working out your decks.

Walkthrough

Back 4 Blood Walkthrough Sections

Searching for a specific walkthrough segment? Snap the connections beneath to leap to...

Back 4 Blood Campaign Walkthrough
Post Hope - Tutorial Introduction

Act 1-The Devil's Return

Resurgence
Passage of Blood
Torment Train
The Crossing

Act 1 - Search and Rescue

A Clean Sweep

Book lovers

Tavern Blitz

Act 1 - The Dark Before the Dawn

Exceptional Delivery

The Diner

Act 1-Blue Dog Hollow

Terrible Seeds

Damnation's Bells

Deserted

The Sound of Thunder

Act 2 - The Armory

A Call to Arms

The Handy Man

Act 2 - Plan B

Line Cleaners

Hinterland
Trailer Trashed
The Clog
The Broken Bird

Act 2 - Job 10:22

Envoy of the Worm Part 1
Envoy of the Worm Part 2
Grave Danger

Act 3 - Dr. Rogers Neighborhood

Farther Afield
Pioneering Trails
Lodges by the Lake
Nursery Party
T-5

Act 3 - Remnants

A Friend in Need
Measuring up
The Road to Hell
The Body Dump

Act 4 - The Abomination

The Abomination

Searching for additional? Look at IGN's Essential Tips and Tricks for Getting Started or even our itemized manual for choosing the Best Cards and Combinations that Back 4 Blood has to bring to the table.

Fortress Hope

Fortress Hope - The Main Hub

At the point when initially beginning, you'll start in Fort Hope, which is viewed as the game's primary center point. From here, you'll approach all that you'll at any point need, regardless of whether it be overseeing supplies, beginning effort missions, altering card decks, or trying out weapons in the shooting range.

While there's no correct way of finishing this region, we have itemized every one of the various exercises you can look at while investigating the region.

Mission Manager

Converse with the Campaign Manager to save a server for your next crusade, picking the beginning point and trouble, or refocusing a past run.

Supplies Manager

Converse with the Supplies Manager to spend Supply Points acquired during efforts and purchase beauty care products, just as cards to use in your deck.

Card Manager

Converse with the Card Manager to make and redo card decks to allow yourself a battling opportunity with your most loved advantages and rewards.

Terminating Range

Head outside of the camp to work on shooting every one of the four kinds of primary weapons: Assault Rifles, Shotguns, Sniper Rifles, and Machine Guns - just as Sidearms, and weapon alterations

Look at our Weapons center point to find out about every weapon that is accessible in-game.

Prepared to get everything rolling on your first Campaign mission? Snap the connection underneath to leap to the main mission in Act 1: The Devil's Return.

Act 1: The Devil's Return

The Devil's Return Walkthrough Sections

Separated into four separate missions, Back 4 Blood's Act 1: The Devil's Return missions can be found beneath. Searching for a specific walkthrough segment? Snap the connections beneath to leap to...

Act 1 - The Devil's Return

Resurgence
Passage of Blood
Torment Train
The Crossing

Searching for additional? Why not look at IGN's Back 4 Blood Essential Tips and Tricks Guide or head back to our Walkthrough Hub to finish much more Campaign Co-Op Missions.

Resurgence

Recorded underneath is the finished Resurgence walkthrough and system guide.
Departure Evansburgh

At the point when you're prepared to begin, open the saferoom entryway and follow the fundamental way as it drives you through a few stories of the high rise until you arrive at the housetop. All through the various floors, you'll experience a few Ridden in both the lobbies and when getting through the additional condo rooms that you're allowed to investigate for provisions.

Whenever you've cleared the Ridden and looked through the additional rooms, your group will wind up on the rooftop.

From here, proceed with the mission by bringing down the extension. After associating with the winch, be cautioned that it will trigger a swarm, so guarantee your group is exceptional prior to proceeding.

You'll need to have your group position themselves by the scaffold, as it'll go about as a channel point, making it simple to take out numerous adversaries immediately as they exit from the structure to which you brought down the extension and the structure to one side.

With the space cleared, advance across and proceed through the structure until you discover a leave point set apart with yellow shower paint.

Drop down to the leave point underneath and take out any Ridden that race into the little region.

When the region is clear, proceed outside to the truck warehouse. You'll need to remain for the most part on top of the trucks and try not to alarm any of the crows that you'll discover dispersed across the terminal - if ineffective, you'll face a few crowds of Ridden, which will scrutinize your group.

In case you were effective in staying away from the crows or have wrapped up getting the region free from the crowds, you'll track down a few enormous cement pipes that are totally piled up towards the finish of the warehouse. Utilize the trucks to move onto the lines above and keep on continuing through the close by entryway.

As you enter, take out the Ridden inside, and you'll discover the saferoom toward the finish of the passage.

The writing is on the wall; you've finished the primary mission of Back 4 Blood. When you're prepared to proceed, you can track down the total walkthrough for the following mission, Tunnel of Blood, while tapping the connection beneath.

Tunnel of Blood Walkthrough

Passage of Blood

Passage of Blood Walkthrough

Recorded beneath is the finished Tunnel of Blood Walkthrough and procedure guide.

Break Evansburgh

When your group is all set, open the protected room entryway and follow the way left, taking out any Ridden en route. As you close to the passage entrance, you'll notice an enormous shine red cloud show up starting from the earliest stage ends up being a goliath Ogre.

Notwithstanding the calls to set out toward the passage, we tracked down that battling the Ogre out in the open was the most straightforward choice, considering that the passages are loaded with normal Ridden, which you'll wind up battling close by the Ogre, making the fight harder than it must be.

So all things considered, what's the most ideal way of overcoming the Ogre? Indeed, initially, you'll need to ensure that you're battling the Ogre with your whole group. Also, similar as all uncommon Ridden, you'll notice that the Ogre has a few light/gleam pink regions around its body - basically on its neck and in its stomach. These regions are known as weakspots, which will bargain altogether more harm than expected when hit.

Alongside exploiting weakspots, you'll need to guarantee that you stay away when battling Ogre's as they have a really huge reach. In case you're inside their arriving at distance, they'll not just swing their arms toward you, managing huge harm, yet they can likewise get you and will continue to crush you - something you'll need to keep away from no matter what.

Beast's likewise can throw enormous wads of goo and guts towards your area. Fortunately the development to this assault is moderately lethargic, so make sure to continue to move and avoid the ball before it arrives at your area, as it'll bargain a lot of harm. Recuperating from the assault isn't moment either, so it will make you helpless against other Ridden until you can recover financially and into the battle.

Whenever you have taken out the Ogre, advance toward the passage and start battling through the Ridden as you head towards the finish of the passage.
Close to the end, you'll track down an entryway along the left divider - head inside.

Subsequent to clearing the provisions room, open the entryway, head to the furthest limit of the way, and turn directly as you head through the red-themed hallway.

Explore the hall and keep following the way - taking out any Ridden en route - until you go over another inventory room and a locked entryway.

At the point when you're prepared to proceed, open the entryway and clear the space of Ridden. While taking out the Ridden, you'll experience one more Ogre, which you'll have to overcome. Like previously, focus on weakspots and try not to be inside its reach. In case you're battling, we recommend returning inside the stockpile room. Not exclusively can it not contact you, however you'll have the option to release however much harm as could reasonably be expected without the danger of getting any harm.

When the region is clear, proceed ahead through the hole toward the finish of the passage.

From here, follow the street left until you go over a huge yellow structure that peruses Shelter on the rooftop. Take out the Ridden around the compound and continue underneath the structure, through the entryway underneath the dazzling red light.

Take out the Ridden stowing away inside the storm cellar and climb the steps to arrive at the protected room.

The writing is on the wall; you've finished the Tunnel of Blood mission. When you're prepared to proceed, click the connection underneath to leap to the following mission, Pain Train.

Pain Train Walkthrough

Torment Train

Torment Train Walkthrough

Recorded beneath is the finished Pain Train Walkthrough and Strategy guide.

Return to Fort Hope

With your group all set, open the saferoom entryway and take out the Ridden meandering the yard and inside the carport.

Remember to check inside the carport for any extra supplies and Copper!

When the region is clear, keep following the way and take out the following flood of Ridden that you experience by the house at the highest point of the slope.

With those dealt with, keep following the way as it drives you through a mist filled bog region. With restricted perceivability, make certain to stay all together and navigate the bog cautiously as you'll discover Ridden wandering all through the space.

Not very far through the marsh, you'll recognize a little homicide of crows on an edge - you'll need to put forth a valiant effort to sneak past them. Lamentably, in the event that you end up alarming the crows, you'll trigger a crowd.

Having endured the bog, hop down the huge edge and take out the Ridden wandering the train carriages.

Whenever you've cleared the region, don't be hesitant to look outside of what might be expected, as you'll discover a lot of Copper and different supplies all through the space.

Since they have been dealt with move ahead through the train yard until you run over a huge turned-over train vehicle.

Discover a Way Over the Train Car

With no real way to over, you'll track down a huge slope inclining toward a bunch of steps close by, which paves the way to a little control room.

Pull together with your group on the subsequent floor - this will give key benefit focuses to give you the advantage over the approaching Ridden - and actuate the control board, which will trigger an enormous swarm of Ridden.

The following are a couple tips and deceives for managing the approaching crowd during this particular experience.

Have somewhere around one colleague center exclusively around the slope, as this will go about as a phenomenal piping point, making it fundamentally simpler to take out various foes on the double.

Should a colleague have an extra Molotov, right now is an ideal opportunity to utilize it! We suggest setting it simply before the turned-over train vehicle, as any Ridden that leap over will be inundated on fire.

With the crowd managed, utilize the hill of rock to move over the train vehicle. Moving ahead, search for the enormous structure to one side and move through the messed up window.

Continue to the Saferoom

Once inside, clear your path through the structure, taking out the Ridden en route - there's only one way you can go - and you'll discover the saferoom at the end subsequent to climbing a huge flight of stairs.

The writing is on the wall; you've finished the Pain Train mission! You can track down a full walkthrough for the following mission, The Crossing, by tapping the connection underneath.

The Crossing

The Crossing Walkthrough

Have you endeavored to finish The Crossing yet keep on bombing each time? Indeed, the guidelines for this specific mission aren't by and large exceptionally clear, so we're here to help. When you better get what you need to do, we ensure that you'll experience no difficulty finishing this mission going ahead.

So you're likely pondering, do you have to get ready for The Crossing any in an unexpected way? All things considered, that is completely dependent upon you and your playing style; notwithstanding, in case you are searching for counsel, we would suggest utilizing Mobility and Defense type Active Cards, as you'll do bunches of running and will take a lot of harm, so extra endurance and wellbeing most certainly wouldn't do any harm.

Before we start, we can not pressure sufficient exactly that speak with your group - particularly so during The Crossing. In the event that you have a crew of companions, you'll probably be fine; nonetheless, in case you're playing with randoms - we were in a comparable situation, so we feel for you - and you're not utilizing voice talk, you'll need to put forth a functioning attempt to use in-game interchanges, for example, pings.

In the event that you're playing with randoms, you'll probably be all around acquainted with groups cleaning once and afterward disbanding - particularly during this specific mission. So while there's not all that much you can do about this, simply attempt to make it happen, as you'll ultimately match with a respectable group.

Step by step instructions to Escape Across the Bridge

When your tidy up group is all set, open the protected room entryway and clear the space of all Ridden, yet ensure that you DO NOT shoot the enormous red fuel tank that is obstructing the way to the scaffold presently.

With the space cleared, do a check for any provisions that you can discover, as you won't get an opportunity to do as such after this point.

With the group prepared, search for the red fuel tank sitting along a huge substantial divider and take shots at it. Following the fuel tank's blast, a swarm of Ridden will storm downward on the space.

Presently, this is the place where many groups turn out badly, as they'll stick around nearby, endeavoring to clear the swarm before they proceed. In any case, there's a trick to this crowd, as it won't stop. So regardless of how long you attempt to endure it, the crowd will simply continue to come.

When the divider has been obliterated, rush across the extension as fast as could really be expected, as the more you hold back to cross, the seriously difficult it will be to endure.

So how would you cross the scaffold? All things considered, it's essential to your group's prosperity that everybody crosses the extension simultaneously. So continue to run towards the waypoint marker somewhere far off, taking out any Ridden hindering your way en route.

Arriving at the finish of the extension, head inside the boat's opening, which can be found by the blue truck, and advance up the close by set of steps to arrive at the top deck.

Collectively, hurry to the furthest edge of the top deck, where you'll track down a white van that has collided with the side of the ship.

Here you'll track down a little way that prompts your recently shown up help group. Head onto the extension and trust that everybody will show up.

When your group has pulled together here and kept on holding off the approaching swarm, get the scaled down weapon that is found on the ground by the substantial square and spot it nearby - do ensure that it is situated such that it can cover the length of the boat, as whenever it is put, you can not pick it back up.

Instructions to Use Explosive to Cut Off the Horde and Blow Up the Boat

Since your group has held the region and set down the smaller than usual weapon, you'll need to establish a few explosives to remove the crowd.

To do this, we energetically suggest running in gatherings of two, so two colleagues will cooperate to establish the bomb in the demonstrated region, while two stay back as they keep on monitoring the swarm.

Defending Team:

If you're remaining back, have one colleague man the small firearm while different draws the consideration of the swarm, bringing them inside prime scope of the smaller than expected weapon. This specific occupation is somewhat clear, so if the bomb group is battling, you might pick to run an extra part in the explosives group for reinforcement without an excessive number of issues.

Explosives Team:

The explosives group is apparently the really difficult job of the two, so you'll need to guarantee that this work is passed on to your two most certain colleagues, as the possibly way you'll succeed is on the off chance that you both have each other's back, taking out any Ridden that could be an expected danger as it's not difficult to become overpowered in the boats now and again restricted living arrangements. So, when you're prepared, get the two explosives by the Humvee and begin advancing towards the two-waypoint marker, which can be found on the least deck of the ship, inside the Engine Room.

If you're battling to discover the waypoint markers, search for the sufficiently bright flights of stairs and drop them until you arrive at the base floor. Whenever you've tracked down the unstable areas, begin establishing them; notwithstanding, you'll need to organize this with your group, as you'll have 60 seconds to get back to your help group on the scaffold; any other way, you'll capitulate to the blast.

On the off chance that your group has figured out how to get back to the extension after effectively planting the explosives, stand by out the rest of the clock as you keep on taking out any approaching Ridden. As the clock runs out, watch as the boat detonates into blazes.

So the writing is on the wall, you've finished the last mission of the principal part in Act 1. Since you've finished The Crossing, it's an ideal opportunity to move onto A Clean Sweep, the primary mission in section two of Act 1.

A Clean Sweep Walkthrough

Searching for significantly more? Why not look at IGN's

Essential Tips and Tricks for Getting Started in Back 4 Blood.

Act_1:_Search_and_Rescue

A Clean Sweep

A Clean Sweep Walkthrough

Recorded beneath is the finished A Clean Sweep Walkthrough and system guide.
Head into Town and Rescue the Survivors

When your group is all set, head out the entryway and advance towards the door. Open it to get into the town.
Clear the Gas Station of Ridden

To one side, you'll detect some Ridden outside the corner store where survivors are being held. Dispense with the Ridden.

Rout the Breaker

Whenever you've managed the smaller than normal multitude, a Breaker will bust through the door of the carport at the corner store.

Regardless of their monstrous size, Breakers are dexterous and quick, ready to jump significant distances and hammer the ground, making a range of impact.

With a lot of wellbeing, you'll need to make a point to take them out as fast as conceivable with your group. Focus on its flimsy points: chest, thigh and behind its shoulder. Continue moving while at the same time managing Breakers to try not to get hit.

Salvage the Survivors in the Liquor Store

Whenever you've taken the Breaker out, plunder around the corner store prior to heading up the street. Go through the rear entryway and battle the Ridden sneaking in its way.

You'll go over a door that should be opened to get into the alcohol store. Press the button close to it. Doing as such will call the Horde, so be prepared.

Try not to remain by the entryway to battle the Horde. All things being equal, flip back around to the principle street for more open space and hold your ground there.

Free the Survivors from the Cocoons

There are four survivors you need to free inside the store. Tune in for the callouts of the survivors to find out about where they're found.

The first can be discovered when you enter the entryway and make a right. Look again to one side in a little room and you'll see the main survivor.

Subsequent to leaving the little room, make a right and walk straight until you see a blue entryway to your left side. You'll track down the second survivor in there.

The third and fourth survivors can be found toward the front of the alcohol store with the racks.

As you leave the alcohol store from where you entered, you'll discover an entryway close to the room where you liberated the main survivor. In the event that you have a tool compartment, feel free to open it for some plunder.

Get to the Library Saferoom

Advance back to the rear entryway. As you proceed with straight, you'll see the saferoom entryway directly before you.

Furthermore, there you go, you've finished A Clean Sweep. When you're prepared, click the connection beneath to leap to the following mission, Book Worms.

Bibliophiles

Book WormsWalkthrough

Recorded beneath is the finished Book

WormsWalkthrough and methodology guide.

Research and Fortify the Library

When you and your group are all set, open the entryway into the library and invigorate it against the ridden.

On the left of your screen, you'll see a clock for "Approaching Horde." Board up the four windows before the clock heads out to keep a multitude of Ridden from entering the library.

Be cautioned that there are as yet Ridden present in the library, so stay alarm and work with your group to kill them.

Here are the areas of the four windows.

The main window will be on a similar floor from which you entered the library. Head past the steps and into the room on the right. You'll see the principal window.

Stronghold sheets are found close to every window, so don't stress over looking for them. Every window must be blocked multiple times, so continue to return to a similar spot to top off on Fortification loads up.

When you leave the room of the primary window, go to one side and head only a few doors down. Go into the room to your right side and make another right. You'll track down the second window with the Fortification Boards close to it.

Leave the two rooms you entered and head left to go up the steps. Continue to go straight and you'll see the third window to your left side past the entryway. Stronghold Boards can be found close to the long work area with the PCs.

The last window is close to the third window. Head out the entryway and look left. The window and Fortification Boards are not too far off.

Ideally, you and your group have blocked all windows before the clock closes.

Salvage the Remaining Survivors and Clear the Hotel of Ridden

By the last window, there's a leave entryway you can take to get outside. Make certain to plunder around the library before you head out as one more clock for an Incoming Horde begins when you open the entryway.

Once outside, you will experience huge loads of Ridden that you'll need to cut through, yet it shouldn't be an issue as the space is quite open.

To get to the lodging, you'll need to get into the rear entryway at the edge of the guide in the middle of a blue house and red structure.

Whenever you've endured the back street, you'll see a flight of stairs driving down with certain explosives obstructing the passageway into the loft. Explode it and advance inside. In any case, be cautious, there are sleepers roosted on the divider. Take them out prior to progressing up the steps.

To one side of the steps, there's an entryway that is available with a toolbox. Go ahead and open it now or prior to leaving the condo.

Advance up to the subsequent floor and go into the primary room to your left side. There may be a Sleeper roosted to one side, so keep an eye out.

Head through the openings in the divider and make the way for track down one more degree of steps. Head up and you'll run over a dull entryway where the survivors are. Approach it and you'll free them.

Plunder whatever you can and advance towards the exit and to the saferoom.

Go through the rear entryway you used to get to the inn and you'll discover the saferoom further up on the left.

Furthermore, there you go, you've finished Book Worms. When you're prepared, click the connection beneath to leap to the following mission, Bar Room Blitz.

Bar Room Blitz Walkthrough

Tavern Blitz

Tavern Blitz Walkthrough

Recorded underneath is the finished Bar Room Blitz Walkthrough and technique guide.

Head to Keet's Bar

At the point when your group is prepared, open the entryway and plunder whatever you find. No adversaries are on the floor of your structure, so go ahead and take as much time as is needed.

When you head down the steps, you'll see a barricade shaped at the base to ward the Ridden off. Jump over the side of the steps to arrive at the base floor and kill the Ridden.

After coming to outside, more Ridden anticipate. Feel free to deal with them and afterward head the truck left close to the fence on the right side close to a blue canvas. Hop on the truck and over the fence to get to Keet's Bar.

Entering Keet's bar, there's tons to plunder, so ensure you do as such.

A tool compartment entryway is open to one side of the bar.

Start the Jukebox to Draw the Horde

At the point when you and your group are prepared, feel free to begin the jukebox.

Be ready to confront a couple floods of Ridden, as the jukebox will occasionally separate and must be fixed if the Ridden harm it.

We recommend every player cover a passageway to the bar and watch every others back as the Ridden will be attracted to the jukebox. Try not to adhere to each other as the swarm can get somewhat overpowering on occasion.

If you or any player in your group has any security fencing, this present time would be a decent opportunity to set them up at the passages.

At the highest point of your screen, you'll see a number that relates to the number of individuals have been stacked onto a transport. There are three transports that must be stacked.

In the event that the jukebox separates, have one individual fix it while the other three spotlight on the Ridden.

Break in the Humvee

After each of the three transports are stacked, every one of you need to clear a path to the humvee that is holding up external the bar.

So the writing is on the wall, you've finished the last mission of the second part in Act 1. Since you've finished Bar Room Blitz, it's an ideal opportunity to move onto Special Delivery, the main mission in section three of Act 1.

Act 1: The Dark Before the Dawn

The Dark Before the Dawn Walkthrough Sections

Separated into two separate missions, Back 4 Blood's Act 1: The Dark Before the Dawn missions can be found beneath. Searching for a specific walkthrough segment? Snap the connections beneath to leap to...

Act 1 - The Dark Before the Dawn

Uncommon Delivery

The Diner

Searching for additional? Why not look at IGN's Back 4 Blood Essential Tips and Tricks Guide or head back to our Walkthrough Hub to finish significantly more Campaign Co-Op Missions.

Uncommon Delivery

Uncommon Delivery Walkthrough

Recorded beneath is the finished Special Delivery Walkthrough and procedure guide.

Head into Town and Search for the Lost Supplies

Leave the saferoom and open the door that heads into town.

From here, you'll need to take out the Ridden prior to progressing towards the stopping point up ahead. Subsequent to killing the Ridden, feel free to plunder around prior to proceeding.

Whenever you're done, advance toward the structure with the red flare. Take out the Ridden inside and clear your path through the structure

Discover and Deliver the Supply Boxes to the Safe Room

After leaving, there's a structure with a tool stash entryway that can be opened.

In this region, you'll need to discover supply boxes and convey them into the protected room. From our playthroughs, the stock boxes can be found in the white truck with the back open, up the steps close to the truck, or on top of a red freight compartment further up the way to one side.

The player(s) holding the inventory box can run, yet can't utilize their weapons, so either drop the case to battle the Ridden or have your group escort you to the saferoom, which is only up ahead.

Advance into the saferoom and spot the stockpile boxes on the table.

Furthermore, there you go, you've finished Special Delivery, a lovely short and basic mission. When you're prepared to proceed, click the connection underneath to leap to the following mission, The Diner.

The Diner

The Diner Walkthrough

Recorded beneath is the finished The Diner Walkthrough and technique guide.

Convey the Supplies to the Diner

At the point when your group has facilitated on who will convey the inventory boxes, open the entryway and advance toward the door, killing any Ridden en route.

To open the entryway, you'll need to press the button, which will bring in the Horde.

Have two individuals look towards the space of the door while the other two peer not too far off as the Ridden advance toward you.

Subsequent to clearing the Ridden, go past the entryway and promptly look to one side. You'll see a tool stash entryway. Feel free to open it in the event that you have a tool stash accessible.

From here, advance up the separated fence and into the structure.

Plunder what you find and clear your path through the structure and to the leave entryway.

In case you're holding an inventory box, feel free to drop it and shoot the Ridden possessing the streets.

Whenever you're done, pick the inventory put away back and head to the burger joint. Spot the stock boxes at its assigned area.

Fix the Generator

Prior to fixing the generator, stock up on ammunition, explosives and different supplies that you see encompassing you. It's there on purpose. When you start the generator, multitudes of Ridden will advance towards you, so be ready.

Pick up the security fencing and set them around the blockades to dial back any Ridden that gets in.

There's likewise a minigun for you to utilize. Mount it in the little post you've recently fabricated and prepare for the fight to come.

Work in twos and center around the wall encompassing the coffee shop. The Ridden will come from the two sides.

At the point when you're prepared, feel free to fix the generator.

Secure the Diner

At the highest point of your screen, you'll see a clock of how long you need to secure the coffee shop. With the tips referenced above, holding down base ought to be simpler. Make sure to load up on ammunition and projectiles should you run out.

In the event that you succeed, a cutscene will play, finishing the mission.

Furthermore, the writing is on the wall, you've finished The Diner. When you're prepared to proceed, click the connection beneath to leap to Bad Seeds, the principal mission in part four of Act 1.

Act 1: Blue Dog Hollow

Blue Dog Hollow Walkthrough Sections

Separated into four separate missions, Back 4 Blood's Act 1: Blue Dog Hollow missions can be found underneath.

Searching for a specific walkthrough area? Snap the connections underneath to leap to...

Act 1: Blue Dog Hollow

Terrible Seeds

Damnation's Bells

Deserted

The Sound of Thunder

Searching for additional? Why not look at IGN's Back 4 Blood Essential Tips and Tricks Guide or head back to our Walkthrough Hub to finish considerably more Campaign Co-Op Missions.

Awful Seeds

Awful Seeds Walkthrough

Recorded beneath is the finished Bad Seeds Walkthrough guide.

Go to the Tunnel Checkpoint

When your group is prepared to take off, open the secondary passage to the burger joint and start advancing down the slope as you head towards the passage designated spot.

While going down the slope, you'll experience a lot of Ridden - both particular and in gatherings. Fortunately, given the rough landscape, most of Ridden can be taken out from above by means of the many stone edges - essentially limiting any danger of being amassed and overpowered.

As you arrive at the lower part of the slope, head left along the sloppy track and keep taking out any Ridden that crosses your way. Stay alert, however, as the space contains a few little trenches that can stow away gatherings of Ridden. Furthermore, the region is additionally fairly hazy and moderately congested, making perceivability a concern. So, stay a tight load with your group and keep all regions checked.

Examine Holland Farm and Destroy the Nest Nodes

Not very long in the wake of passing by the wooden scaffold, you'll see that the way prompts a homestead that is finished with a huge house and two all around estimated outbuildings.

At the huge house, you'll discover some plunder, just as a toolbox entryway. Feel free to open it on the off chance that you have a toolbox accessible.

As you start researching the Holland Farm, you'll probably experience a few enormous Nest Nodes - while their areas will change contingent upon your run, we frequently viewed the Nest Nodes to be situated inside the two outbuildings and behind the farmhouse.

Need some additional assistance? Look at our total aide on How to Find and Destroy Nests.

This is the place where things can get somewhat interesting and will require key correspondence inside your group as obliterating each Nest Node will trigger a crowd of Ridden. So it's not just significant that your group is good to go, however that you just annihilate each Nest Node in turn as setting off more than one will probably see you rapidly becoming overpowered.

Annihilate the last Nest Node to free the Trailer

When your group has annihilated each of the Nest Nodes around the ranch, follow the waypoint marker to the imploded span close by, where you'll track down the last Nest Node, which you'll have to obliterate to free the trailer. Simply be cautioned, annihilating this last

Nest Node will trigger one more crowd of Ridden.

Get Across the River

With the crowd approaching, finish the waterway back the homestead, by the enormous moved feed bundles, until you track down an opening in the fence that leads across the stream.

Proceed to the Saferoom

When you're across the waterway, follow the waypoint marker up the back road, where you'll track down the protected room inside a little trailer.

The writing is on the wall; you've finished the Bad Seeds mission! On the off chance that your group is prepared to proceed, click the connection beneath to leap to the following story mission, Hell's Bells.

Damnation's Bells

Damnation's BellsWalkthrough

Recorded underneath is the finished Hell's BellsWalkthrough and Strategy guide.
Get to the Church

With your group prepared, leave the trailer and start clearing your path through the passage as you travel towards the Church.

As you've likely generally expected, the passage is loaded with Ridden that you'll have to clear. While it's both dim and fairly confined, we prescribe adhering to the tops of vehicles, as this will give you a greatly improved visual of any approaching Ridden.

Clean the Trailer off of the Road

In the wake of advancing out of the passage, proceed ahead and take out any Ridden nearby. When clear, head over to the back of the huge blue tow truck and utilize the keypad to turn it on and pull the trailer that is obstructing the street upstanding. Simply be cautioned, actuating the tow truck will call the swarm, so be certain that your group is completely ready for the approaching Ridden.

Proceed to the Church

When the trailer is upstanding, move from the opening in its side and finish the way the gulley and damp burial ground as you advance towards the Church.

Continue to adhere to one side of the burial ground, and at last, you'll discover a tool compartment entryway concealed on the mountain.

This way is moderately clear, so as long as you take out any Ridden you experience, stay on the fundamental path, and remain all together, you ought to have practically zero issues arriving at the Church.

Sustain the Church Against the Ridden

After arriving at the congregation, head inside collectively and start getting the wooden boards from the heaps dispersed across the floor. Utilize these boards on the windows to fire barricading them to keep any Ridden from getting inside. Whenever you've blocked the windows and cleared any Ridden, you'll have finished the Hell's Bells mission.

Since your group is prepared to proceed, click on the accompanying connect to leap to the following mission, Abandoned.

Deserted

Deserted Walkthrough

Recorded underneath is the finished Abandoned walkthrough and technique guide.

Get to the Mine Saferoom

At the point when prepared, leave the Church and start following the way until you run over the back access to a corner store. Clear the region and continue to open the entryway, and clear your path through the service station and out to the primary street ahead.

From here, move ahead collectively and clear the Ridden from the street region - take a stab at utilizing the top of the huge semi-trailer to get a stature advantage on the Ridden, as this should make it simpler to bring them down.

When clear, proceed to the furthest limit of the street and turn left. Follow this street as far as possible - dealing with any Ridden en route - and you'll track down a huge red house to your right side.

Ascend the radiant yellow stepping stool on the shed close to the house and continue to enter through the wrecked window.

Obliterate the Nest to Proceed

Once inside, you'll need to obliterate the Nest Nodes to proceed. Similar as in the past, annihilating the Nest Nodes will call the crowd. So just take out each Nest Node in turn and guarantee that your group is prepared for the invasion of Ridden that will be coming your direction right away. While everything relies upon your group and your playing style, we prescribe remaining inside the house to manage the crowd.

We found that remaining on the subsequent floor and utilizing any semblance of the flight of stairs to make a pipe framework. In case you're remaining at the top, you'll be in prime situation to take out any Ridden endeavoring to arrive at the highest point of the steps. Simply be cautioned, Ridden will enter through the messed up windows that can be found on the subsequent floor, so ensure you have your colleagues covering these regions to forestall being brought forth from behind.

Proceed Through Blue Dog Village

When the house is clear, proceed out the rear of the house and continue to lift the yellow vehicle that is impeding the way to the Blue Dog Saferoom - you'll discover a keypad that actuates the Tow Truck close to its back.

From here, move through the recently opened hole in the divider and proceed ahead in an orderly fashion as you evade and keep away from the Ridden. At last, toward the stopping point, you'll discover a house - enter through the entryway, and you'll come to wellbeing.

Climb Old Blue Dog Mine Trail and Enter the Saferoom

Subsequent to getting the house free from all provisions, exit out the rear of the house and clear any Ridden that you find meandering over the gulley, past the lawn. When clear, move across the log and enter the Old Blue Dog Mine Trail.

As you start rising the mine path, you'll regularly experience Mine Shacks along the edge of the way. Point and shoot the strategically located hazardous barrels that can be found at the passageway to the shacks to prevent any Ridden from getting away from them.

Collectively, keep on rising the mine path as you climb the old metal shafts. At the top, you'll discover a leave that drives you up another soil way, which you'll have to follow until you gone over a huge metal mining shaft.

We propose getting a move on during this specific part of the mission, as it's not important to kill each Ridden that you experience. All things being equal, attempt just killing the Ridden that endeavor to obstruct your way as you climb the Old Blue Dog mine path.

As you climb the path, pay special mind to a little shed that has a tool stash entryway. On the off chance that you've dealt with the Ridden and have some extra time, open the entryway with a toolbox to get some plunder.

Once came to, proceed up the flights of stairs, taking out any Ridden en route that endeavor to hinder your way, and you'll discover the saferoom at the extremely top.

The writing is on the wall; you've effectively finished the Abandoned mission. To proceed to the following and last mission of Act 1: Blue Dog Hollow, click the connection beneath.

The Sound of Thunder

The Sound of Thunder Walkthrough

Burden the Howitzer with Ammo

When your group is all set, open the protected room entryway and proceed down the mining tunnel until you arrive at an enormous open region by the mine passage - make certain to deal with any Ridden en route.

When you arrive at the huge open region, your fundamental focal point of this mission will be to annihilate the mine passage. To do as such, head towards the Howitzer - which can be found towards the center of the space.

Once more, correspondence is basic all through this mission as the Ridden will persistently enter the site, regardless of the number of you kill. Therefore, you'll need to play out the level headed as fast as could be expected, all while having your group deal with any Ridden that close to the Howitzer.

Fire the Howitzer and Destroy the Mine Entrance

With everybody set up, start getting the rockets from the box on the ground and burden them into the Howitzer. Once stacked, fire the rocket into the mine passageway and rehash until all rockets have been stacked and dispatched.

Departure in the Humvee

In the wake of terminating the last rocket, watch as the mine passageway breakdowns. After falling, search for the Humvee that is situated towards the right of the space and move inside to end the last mission of Act 1: Blue Dog Hollow.

Congrats! You've completed the primary demonstration of Back 4 Blood. Presently it's an ideal opportunity to continue on to the primary part of Act 2: A Call to Arms. Snap the connection beneath to peruse the walkthrough for A Call to Arms.

Act 2: Plan B

Plan B Walkthrough Sections

Separated into five separate missions, Back 4 Blood's Act 2: Plan B missions can be found beneath. Searching for a specific walkthrough segment? Snap the connections beneath to leap to...

Act 2 - Plan B

Line Cleaners
Hinterland
Trailer Trashed
The Clog
The Broken Bird

Searching for additional? Why not look at IGN's Back 4 Blood Essential Tips and Tricks Guide or head back to our Walkthrough Hub to finish significantly more Campaign Co-Op Missions.

Step by step instructions to Guides

Back 4 Blood How-To Guides

Searching for something specifically? Snap the connections beneath to leap to...

How to Escape Across the Bridge and Blow Up the Boat
How to Find and Destroy Nests
Step by step instructions to Escape Across the Bridge and Blow Up the Boat

Have you endeavored to finish The Crossing however keep on flopping each time? Indeed, the guidelines for this specific mission aren't actually exceptionally clear, so we're here to help. When you better get what you need to do, we ensure that you'll experience no difficulty finishing this mission going ahead.

So you're likely pondering, do you have to get ready for The Crossing any in an unexpected way? All things considered, that is altogether dependent upon you and your playing style; in any case, in case you are searching for counsel, we would suggest utilizing Mobility and Defense type Active Cards, as you'll do loads of running and will take a lot of harm, so extra endurance and wellbeing certainly wouldn't do any harm.

Before we start, we can not pressure sufficient exactly that speak with your group - particularly so during The Crossing. On the off chance that you have a crew of companions, you'll probably be fine; in any case, in case you're playing with randoms - we were in almost the same situation, so we feel for you - and you're not utilizing voice visit, you'll need to put forth a functioning attempt to use in-game interchanges like pings.

On the off chance that you're playing with randoms, you'll probably be all around intimately acquainted with groups cleaning once and afterward disbanding - particularly during this specific mission. So while there's not all that much you can do about this, simply attempt to make it happen, as you'll ultimately match with a good group.

The most effective method to Escape Across the Bridge

When your tidy up group is all set, open the protected room entryway and clear the space of all Ridden, yet ensure that you DO NOT shoot the enormous red fuel tank that is hindering the way to the extension right now.

With the space cleared, do a check for any provisions that you can discover, as you won't get an opportunity to do as such after this point.

With the group prepared, search for the red fuel tank sitting along an enormous substantial divider and take shots at it. Following the fuel tank's blast, a swarm of Ridden will storm downward on the space.

Presently, this is the place where many groups turn out badly, as they'll stick around nearby, endeavoring to clear the swarm before they proceed. In any case, there's a trick to this crowd, as it won't stop. So regardless of how long you attempt to endure it, the crowd will simply continue to come.

When the divider has been annihilated, rush across the

scaffold as fast as could really be expected, as the more you hold on to cross, the seriously difficult it will be to endure.

So how would you cross the extension? Indeed, it's pivotal to your group's prosperity that everybody crosses the extension simultaneously. So continue to run towards the waypoint marker somewhere out there, taking out any Ridden impeding your way en route.

Arriving at the finish of the scaffold, head inside the boat's opening, which can be found by the blue truck, and advance up the close by set of steps to arrive at the top deck.

Collectively, rush to the furthest edge of the top deck, where you'll track down a white van that has collided with the side of the ship.

Here you'll track down a little way that prompts your recently shown up help group. Head onto the extension and trust that everybody will show up.

When your group has refocused here and kept on holding off the approaching crowd, get the little weapon that is found on the ground by the substantial square and spot it nearby - do ensure that it is situated such that it can cover the length of the boat, as whenever it is set, you can not pick it back up.

Step by step instructions to Use Explosive to Cut Off the Horde and Blow Up the Boat

Since your group has held the region and set down the smaller than normal weapon, you'll need to establish a few explosives to remove the crowd.

To do this, we energetically suggest running in gatherings of two, so two colleagues will cooperate to establish the bomb in the demonstrated region, while two stay back as they keep on monitoring the swarm.

Defending Team:

If you're remaining back, have one colleague man the smaller than expected firearm while different draws the consideration of the crowd, bringing them inside prime scope of the scaled down weapon. This specific occupation is generally direct, so if the bomb group is battling, you might select to run an extra part in the explosives group for reinforcement without an excessive number of issues.

Explosives Team:

The explosives group is apparently the seriously difficult job of the two, so you'll need to guarantee that this work is passed on to your two most sure colleagues, as the possibly way you'll succeed is on the off chance that you both have each other's back, taking out any Ridden that could be an expected danger as it's not difficult to become overpowered in the boats once in a while restricted living arrangements.

With that said, when you're prepared, get the two explosives by the Humvee and begin advancing towards the two-waypoint marker, which can be found on the most reduced deck of the ship, inside the Engine Room.

If you're battling to discover the waypoint markers, search for the sufficiently bright flights of stairs and plummet them until you arrive at the base floor. Whenever you've tracked down the touchy areas, begin establishing them; in any case, you'll need to arrange this with your group, as you'll have 60 seconds to get back to your help group on the extension; if not, you'll surrender to the blast.

In the event that your group has figured out how to get back to the extension after effectively establishing the explosives, stand by out the rest of the clock as you keep on taking out any approaching Ridden. As the clock runs out, watch as the boat detonates into blazes.
So the writing is on the wall, you've finished the last mission of the main part in Act 1.

Searching for much more? Why not look at IGN's Essential Tips and Tricks for Getting Started in Back 4

Blood.

Instructions to Find and Destroy Nests

Back 4 Blood highlights various targets that players should finish on their central goal as Cleaners to overcome the Ridden, yet not all will be clear. This page contains data on the most proficient method to discover and annihilate Ridden Nests that can hinder your advancement.

Beginning in Act 2, you'll regularly be met with road obstructions in your movement from enormous odd developments that show up in houses and different regions, covering regions and hindering you from pushing ahead. In these areas, you might see your target shift to "annihilate the homes" to continue.

The most effective method to Find Nests

In the vast majority of these circumstances, the developments and mass of rings made by the Ridden will all middle at one point, typically a hindered entryway, span, or other chokepoint. It is from this space you should start your inquiry.

Look along the ground from this essential issue for various sparkling red ringlets that snake along the ground like links, and move out collectively to find every one. These delicately sparkling rings will consistently end in a little region that has one more mass of development, with huge pustule-like shining spheres. Obliterating these circles is your way of pushing ahead, yet it will not without result.

Step by step instructions to Destroy Nests

Whenever you have found one (of a few) ringlets finishing in a home site with the enormous pustules, signal your group and let them in on you are going to annihilate that specific ring. Doing as such will trigger a little yet not unimportant swarm of Ridden, so you ought to consistently be prepard to fall back and safeguard a point with the remainder of your group until the space is generally peaceful.

When the crowd is cleared out, move onto the following ring and rehash the interaction until all the diverse home destinations are annihilated, and the way ahead will at long last be accessible.

Try not to attempt to annihilate a few home locales immediately - this won't join into only one crowd assault, however will make at least two separate swarms assault you without a moment's delay, and may demonstrate a lethal choice in the event that you become overpowered by assaults from various points.

Best Cards and Combinations Guide

Back 4 Blood - 7 Deck Building Tips From the Developers

Searching for something explicit? Snap the connection beneath to leap to...

Best Active Cards

Best Active Card Combinations

Think you have a superior card blend or have an undisputed top choice that you can't play without? Remember to share your works in the remark segment beneath.

The Best Cards and Card Combinations in Back 4 Blood

Before you go choosing your cards, note that the request where you place your cards in the deck is pivotal, as it can have an immense effect on your in general ongoing interaction experience. The justification for this being that cards put at the highest point of the deck will be given to you before in your run, gone against to simply pulling from the deck haphazardly.

All things considered, the cards at the highest point of the deck will consistently be pulled first, with the primary card of the deck continually being your beginning card. It is consequently, that you ought to consistently put your most significant must-have cards toward the start of the deck, with your lesser wanted cards towards the base portion of the deck.

Best Active Cards to Consider in Back 4 Blood

Recorded underneath, we have point by point probably the best Active Cards to think about utilizing in Back 4 Blood. These cards have been recorded in no specific request.

Before we go any further, it is worth focusing on that the accompanying cards and blends are simply emotional and depend on our own decisions, playstyle, and in general experience that we got during the Back 4 Blood Beta.

Additional opportunity

Card Name: Second Chance

Card Type: Defense

Card Description: + 1 Extra Life and + 10 Health

Let's be honest, Back 4 Blood isn't by and large simple and is known to have especially testing minutes, even on simpler trouble settings - we're taking a gander at you, The Crossing.

All things considered, we strongly suggest running Second Chance, as an additional a life could be the contrast between your group cleaning or simply scratching through. While it's all conviction, we accept that running the Second Chance card is an absolute necessity have card when taking on more testing challenges as the extra wellbeing and additional life could be a finished lifeline - in a real sense.

Prevalent Cardio

Card Name: Superior Cardio

Card Type: Mobility

Card Description: +20% Stamina, + 20% Sprint Efficiency and + 5 Health

One thing you'll rapidly learn is that Back 4 Blood has A LOT of running. So regardless of whether you're essentially running between areas or endeavoring to get away from an approaching crowd of Ridden, the Superior Cardio card is an unquestionable requirement have for any player that regularly winds up moving about and running out of endurance.

All things considered, the special reward of expanded Health and Sprint Efficiency will make getting away from those precarious circumstances a total breeze.

Ridden Slayer

Card Name:Ridden Slayer

Card Type: Offense

Card Description: +35 Weakspot Damage

It's not difficult to get overpowered by Ridden in Back 4 Blood, that is the reason we regularly exploit The Ridden card. With a +35% Weakspot Damage, it's a hard card to miss as this additional harm lift could be a distinct advantage for those that are battling with the approaching extraordinary tainted among the swarms. The quicker you can kill those bigger sort adversaries, the less harm you'll possibly take and the almost certain you'll be to endure.

Reload Drills

Card Name: Reload Drills

Card Type: Offense

Card Description: +30% Reload Speed

At the point when initially beginning, Reload Drills is an incredible card to consider as your deck will probably be extremely restricted, so you'll need to zero in on building a deck that uses your most gainful rewards almost immediately. With the card offering a huge 30% expansion in your reload speed, you'll have less vacation between shots, yet it likewise permits you to invest more energy shooting - something you'll need to exploit during your initial missions.

Best Active Card Combinations

Each card you find and pick can regularly be extraordinary all alone for certain playstyles, however there are a couple of cards that have significantly more noteworthy advantages when working off one another. See the segments beneath for certain instances of incredible Card Combinations

Battle Knife + Battle Lust

Benefit: Knife Bash and Melee Kills Restore 2 Health
The most noteworthy part about the Combat Knife and Battle Lust combo is these will show up in your beginning bunch of cards, so you can utilize this combo first thing while at the same time attempting to get Supply Points to open more cards.

Combat Knife will trade out your slam assault for a blade that can typically kill an ordinary Ridden in a solitary strike, making it a phenomenal Starter Card, and incredible for taking out solitary shambling targets, polishing off strays, and preserving ammunition. When joined with Battle Lust, all scuffle kills will give you 2 Health back - and this applies to your Combat Knife, not simply skirmish weapons that supplant sidearms. Utilizing the previously mentioned strategies, you would now be able to recapture lost wellbeing rapidly by cutting normal Ridden - insofar as you're not getting amassed. Regardless of whether you do get mobbed, this combo implies you'll have the option to get a little wellbeing back while reloading weapons as you can continue assaulting during reloads!

Looking for additional? Look at our Back 4 Blood Beginner's Guide, just as our nitty gritty rundown of Essential Tips and Tricks to Help You Get Started.

Card System

Remember to look at our other card related pages that cover everything from Active Cards, Corruption Cards, and surprisingly more by tapping the connections beneath:

Active Cards
Corruption Cards
Best Cards and Combinations Guide

How Does the Card System Work in Back 4 Blood

Every player will start with a little arrangement of cards remembered for a premade deck that is utilized during the game. These cards will buff your person (and here and there the whole group!) with various inactive or dynamic impacts that are broadly run, and shift from exceptionally situational to plain close to home inclination.

Alongside your starter card drawn toward the start of the mission, you'll will pick one of a few cards in your deck toward the start of each level in an Act. On the off chance that you decide to begin playing later in an Act, you'll have the option to attract more cards to redress, and if your group bombs a level, you'll find the opportunity to attract an extra card to help your next endeavor.

They key to your group's endurance might lie in these cards, so consider cautiously concerning what benefits you need to recieve and how they'll help both you and the group. Attempt and blend cards that help your playstyle with cards that assist you with satisfying a job for your group, and you can even make custom decks for every sort of job.

As you complete levels in an Act, you'll procure Supply Points (more in the event that you complete the targets of the level's Corruption Card, such as coming to the Safe Room with everybody), which can be spent on Supply Line awards back at Fort Hope to purchase all the more remarkable cards with considerably more noteworthy advantages.

Note: Keep a nearby eye out when investigating levels for Intelligence Files, as they can either give everybody in the group a free arbitrary card, or the opportunity to purchase a particular card utilizing cash collected during the Act. In any case, these cards just keep going for the length of your mission, and are not forever added to your deck.

You can just have 15 cards in a deck absolute, and in the event that you have less or begin to run out, you'll be presented to draw irregular cards that can expand your endurance, ammunition, wellbeing, or speed - and can even be stacked on numerous occasions!

Why Card Order Matters When Creating a Deck

Before you select your cards and make a deck, note that the request wherein you place your cards in the deck is essential, as it can fundamentally affect your by and large interactivity experience. This is on the grounds that cards set at the highest point of the deck will be given to you before in your run, instead of simply pulling from the deck arbitrarily.

The cards at the highest point of the deck will consistently be pulled first; nonetheless, the deck's first card is forever your beginning card. Thus, you ought to consistently put your generally significant, must-have cards toward the start of the deck, with your lesser wanted cards or ones that are dependant in your group's circumstance towards the base half as they will be pulled a lot later down the track.

The Complete Back 4 Blood Beginner's Guide

With regards to multiplayer undertakings, scarcely any approach the mystical equation of Left 4 Dead. Nonetheless, with the eventual fate of that specific establishment dead in the water (for the present), Turtle Rock Studios is wanting to fill the hole with Back 4 Blood. Regardless of whether you are a prepared zombie executioner or another Cleaner pursuing the apocalypse, here's beginning and end you need to know with Geek Culture's Complete Back 4 Blood Beginner's Guide!

Back 4 Blood Release Date and Story

Initially postponed from 22 June 2021, we can anticipate getting the world free from the Ridden come this 12 October 2021.

Occurring after a cataclysmic flare-up, the majority of humankind has either been killed or tainted. The animals, presently known as the Ridden, meander the world and represent a threat to every living thing. A gathering of Veterans, known as the Cleaners, are returning together to take what is left of our reality. That is the place where you come in.

Interactivity Overview

From the off, you need to realize that Back 4 Blood is a

simply multiplayer undertaking. Indeed, even alone, you will have bots that can take care of you, yet nothing beats having genuine human players in the interest of personal entertainment.

With regards to online community play, players will be in groups of four, while it can go up to eight players in PvP. Split-screen multiplayer won't be upheld at dispatch, yet it very well might be something to anticipate later on. Crossplay is empowered, so PC and control center players can partake in the game together, even in the Back 4 Blood beta.

Back 4 Blood likewise includes a featuring card framework, with each match permitting players to fabricate a 15-card deck. This deck will contain different lifts and modifiers, permitting you to surrender yourself a leg during various experiences in the game.

Then again, the Ridden have defilement cards that will move things in support of themselves. This can incorporate extraordinary foes, climate impacts, and are controlled by the Game Director, the AI that screens players and change the game to keep things fascinating.

Manual for Surviving Back 4 Blood Beta

In case you are perusing this now, the early see of the Back 4 Blood open beta would have been finished. All things considered, the world is allowed to hop in and have a good time as a component of the open beta which runs from 12 to 16 August.

You will gain admittance to two PvP maps, two center guides, and the Fort Hope people group center point. In any case, everything counts to no end in the event that you can't endure, and to do that, you will require some assistance. This is the place where our total Back 4 Blood novice's aide will help.

Planning for the Hunt

At the point when you initial leap into the Back 4 Blood beta, you will wind up in Fort Hope. This center point region will be the place where you can look at the terminating range, see the forthcoming unlockables that are accessible, form your deck, and show things out for PvE or PvP.

The shooting reach will be a decent spot to begin, assisting you with becoming acclimated to how weapons discharge, their pace of discharge, and how they handle. Every weapon accompanies its own remarkable characteristics, yet by the day's end, you simply need the best weapon to suit your playstyle with regards to popping Ridden heads. You can absolutely do that as you appreciate Back 4 Blood, yet the terminating range is a decent spot to look at things as well.

Make sure to likewise check your deck for the current cards that are in the open beta. With the various lifts, abilities, and rewards, make certain to see how you need to play, and how you may squeeze into your group, be it with companions or with public matchmaking.

Backing players will do well with more projectiles, gauzes, and medical aid units. In case you are centered around killing, expanding your ammunition count and lessening reloading speeds are guaranteed. While the quantity of cards is restricted for the open beta, it gives you a smart thought of what's in store later on and bear the cost of players the adaptability to test.

With all of that set up, you can begin lining up for your initial introduction to the internet based center universe of the Back 4 Blood beta.

General Tips and Tricks

Turn up the sound! Sound signs can tell you where foes are, and permit your group to prepare.

Hearing great additionally reaches out to interchanges with your group. Conversing with one another is consistently a decent way of expanding your odds of endurance. Focus on adversaries, share redesigns and supplies, and holler on the off chance that you need to have some time off and investigate.

Synergise your cards! Stacking endurance or ammunition lifts can go far in giving you a decent beginning, and make forthcoming experiences simpler.

Coordinate your weapons. Ensure not every person is searching for a similar ammunition, and you will make some better memories pushing ahead.

Damage comes in two structures in Back 4 Blood – ordinary and injury harm. The previous can be recuperated utilizing gauzes and medkits, while injury harm requires emergency treatment stations, which are likley found behind supply reserves. Painkillers give a brief fix to injury harm.

Whenever allowed the opportunity, make certain to buy toolboxs. This open up admittance to secret regions that contain important assets, for example, the previously mentioned emergency treatment stations.

Battle Tips and Tricks

Facing the Ridden, going it single-handedly is a reliable catastrophe waiting to happen. Adhere to your group, convey, and don't be an activity saint!

Since the group is the key here, make certain to pay special mind to that cordial fire. Regardless of whether it isn't so generous, harm adds up, so make certain to watch where you fire.

Always use your sidearm and save valuable ammunition for your essential weapons. The force of essential weapons are incredible, however it implies nearly nothing on the off chance that you don't have the ammunition. Sidearms have a lot of extra ammunition lying around, so remember about them.

Be watching out for ecological guides, for example, very much positioned gas canisters. Shoot them and partake in the huge blast.

Most of the foes have gleaming weakspots, so according to video game rationale, focus on these spaces and arrangement additional harm.

Reloading is vital, however when risk approaches, you can skirmish to drive the Ridden away AND not interfere with your reloading.

If you are utilizing a throwable, a red region will be shown to demonstrate its impact span. Avoid companions and focus on the undead.

Prioritise the risky foes, manage bigger targets like

Tallboy or Stingers, as they can undoubtedly crash groups whenever left unattended to.

You will discover weapons during your experiences, and better extraordinariness weapons will consistently have better details. Supplant your beginning weapon at the earliest opportunity. Weapons additionally accompany supportive mods. Should you track down a red-shaded mod, make certain to supplant them with new mods.

Manual for Understanding the Back 4 Blood World

The perils are not just the Ridden, make certain to pay special mind to groups of birds. In the event that you frighten them, they will alarm any close by swarms and ruin your day.

Keep your eyes out for relevant pieces of information, as they will stop for a minute to anticipate. Signs can highlight alerts that have been set, so be extra mindful so as to check around the climate.

Grab each Intel Folder you see, as they can either remunerate you with a free dynamic ccard, or permit you to spend coins to get an all the more impressive reward.

Speaking of coins, scavage around prior to leaving a region. The more cash you have, the more your spending power when the circumstance emerges. Having a partner with the card to detect coins can be very valauble.

As much as could be expected, get the strategic position. Back 4 Blood really gives players greater mobility, so bounce and climb your direction to wellbeing.

The writing is on the wall, Geek Culture's finished novices guide for Back 4 Blood. Albeit this may just apply to the Back 4 Blood open beta now, it will prove to be useful when the game dispatches in October as well. By getting the training in now, you will be vastly improved later on.

Back 4 Blood: Tips And Tricks For Beginners

Back 4 Blood is a game that highly esteems its helpful perspectives, particularly with regards to its maverick light framework that makes "outrageous replayability" in the mission mode. As of late, the entire Rogue-like kind has filled quickly in fame. That term is regularly connected with troublesome ongoing interaction and frustratingly finished runs. This aide will assist you with forestalling early crashes for your runs, yet in addition better you as a player.

Try not to adhere to a fundamental

This one goes out to every one individuals who might not have committed gatherings to play in. Chances are in the event that you have one primary, they may be picked. It's in every case great to represent considerable authority in a class-based game so you know the intricate details of your jobs, however once in a while it may very well be taken. Fundamental in some measure more than one person so your chances are a ton lower in having a person you need taken.

Realize what turns out best for your group

Let's assume you need to principle somebody like Holly. She's a skirmish class who dominates close by other people battle, particularly when she has something like a club or cleaver available. Try not to get an expert marksman with her. She'll scarcely profit from it. Realize what kinds of things turn out best for your group so you can make the most out of their passives and advantages!

Find out more about the card framework

The card framework is an exceptional bend on the roguelike kind in Back 4 Blood. Consider it your assemble. You'll have cards that can support your endurance, development speed, injury opposition, wellbeing, and numerous different advantages. Preferably, you'd need to make or fabricate a deck for each character. That way, you can practice what can turn out best for that particular job.

Obviously, in case you're simply beginning, your deck will be exceptionally restricted and essential. Relax. With the roguelike framework set up, your ensuing runs will just make you more mindful of what works best with the characters you use. You'll ultimately open more cards to add onto your decks en route.

Give careful consideration of what Corruption Cards are played before each mission as well! A small bunch of them will constrain you to play a specific way given their modifiers.

Never stray away from your partners

Back 4 Blood is a game with regards to making due through huge loads of Ridden and crashing through them to finish your targets. Try not to be the legend of your gathering figuring you can rush into a crowd of them. Chances are, you'll be amazingly overpowered and probably debilitated, leaving the remainder of your partners with essentially less capability to manage the current risk.

Try not to start battles until everybody is prepared

You're clearing your path through a level and see a group of birds or a vehicle with a potential caution on it. Try not to make unreasonable clamor on the off chance that you can stay away from a superfluous fight, particularly if a colleague is additionally very nearly kicking the bucket and is attempting to fix themselves up. Envision getting into a goliath battle and the principal foe that surfaces on you downs you on the grounds that a partner didn't consider checking if every other person is prepared. That is simply inconsiderate!

Try not to denounce any kind of authority

This doesn't have any significant bearing in the event that you play on the Recruit trouble. On the Veteran and Nightmare challenges, agreeable fire is empowered. Don't purposely shoot or cut at your partners. You're simply going to make things harder for the remainder of your group and cost the gathering a proceed or even the whole run.

Try not to be voracious

In case you're the superstar who has a strong loadout and some money to save, help out in purchasing things at the protected house for partners. It'll assist with reinforcing the group's general productivity with regards to enduring and bringing down the Ridden. Purchasing your colleague that an additional one prescription pack or explosive may have a significant effect between finishing a mission and cleaning. The equivalent goes with ammunition. Try not to get shotgun shells in case you're shaking a gun and an attack rifle. Another person may utilize it.

Deal with your recuperating

Preferably, you'd need to move toward a battle as ready as could be expected. Whenever a major battle has closed and your group is searching for weapons and different things, you'll occasionally discover a few curatives. This goes a piece inseparably with not being avaricious. Ensure everybody is mended to or near full wellbeing prior to taking those extra medications. Everybody having full wellbeing allows the group a higher opportunity of surviving the ordeal.

Have an approach

You're clearing your path through a situation and see that the climate is set up in a manner for a major fight to happen. Plan out with your partners where you'll perhaps roost up to battle the Ridden. Don't simply go out in the open and give yourselves an ecological inconvenience. Envision starting a major battle against the ridden and you've totally become encircled from every one of the four regions. Well that is the thing that prompts a group wipe.

Help each other out

Utilize recuperating things on each other on the off chance that you see your colleagues fall under a specific limit of wellbeing. Try not to be parsimonious and hush up about all the curatives when you're fit as a fiddle. Likewise, be watching out for things left off in an unexpected direction. Once in a while you'll discover things like free cards and mystery rooms that can be gotten to with a tool stash.

Spend your copper admirably

Copper is the cash you use to spend on prescription stations and the Safe Houses before each mission. You'll essentially purchase new weapons, connections, and stuff like explosives and prescription packs utilizing it. Continuously have some extra copper available for individuals who might be short a couple.

Back 4 Blood is out now in early access for Ultimate Edition buyers. The game will be out for every other person on October 12, 2021. You can get this game on PlayStation 4 and 5, Xbox One and Series S/X, and PC through Steam and Epic Games. To look at more data on Back 4 Blood like news, directs, and surprisingly a forthcoming audit, click here.

www.ingramcontent.com/pod-product-compliance
Lightning Source LLC
LaVergne TN
LVHW010459160826
845677LV00012B/2557

* 9 7 9 8 4 9 4 6 6 1 1 2 8 *